D1442162

animals**animals**

Turtles and Tortoises

by **Renee C. Rebman**

 Marshall Cavendish
Benchmark
New York

For my niece, Laura Ann Zajack

Series consultant:
James C. Doherty
General Curator, Bronx Zoo, New York

Marshall Cavendish Benchmark
99 White Plains Road
Tarrytown, New York 10591-9001
www.marshallcavendish.us

Text copyright © 2007 by Marshall Cavendish Corporation
Illustrations copyright © 2007 by Marshall Cavendish Corporation
Map copyright © 2007 by Marshall Cavendish Corporation
Map by Chistopher Santoro

All Internet sites were available and accurate when sent to press.

Library of Congress Cataloging-in-Publication Data
Rebman, Renee C., 1961-
Turtles and tortoises / by Renee Rebman.
p. cm.—(Animals, animals)
Summary: "Describes the physical characteristics, behavior, habitat, and endangered status of turtles and tortoises"—
Provided by publisher.
Includes bibliographical references and index.
ISBN-13: 978-0-7614-2239-6
ISBN-10: 0-7614-2239-0
1. Turtles—Juvenile literature. 2. Testudinidae—Juvenile literature. I. Title. II. Series.
QL666.C5R33 2006
597.92'4–dc22
2005025612

Photo research by Joan Meisel

Cover photo: Ed Reschke/Peter Arnold, Inc.

The photographs in this book are used by permission and through the courtesy of:
Corbis: 1, Staffan Widstrand; 14, David A. Northcott; 18, Gary Bell/Zefa; 34, Lynda Richardson;
Peter Arnold, Inc.: 7, Thomas Roettir;20, Aldo Brando; 28, Kelvin Aitkin; 30, James Gerholdt; 32,
John Cancalosi; 33, Ed Reschke; 38, Fred Bruemmer; 41, Steve Kaufman; *Photo Researchers, Inc.:* 4, Kenneth H. Thomas;
6, Karl H. Switak; 8, Joseph T. Collins; 9, Anthony Bannister; 10, John Cancalosi; 12, Charles V. Angelo; 15,
Tom McHugh; 16, Michael Patrick O'Neill; 22, Jerry L. Ferrara; 23, Matthew Oldfield, Scuba Zoo; 24, E. R. Degginger; 26,
William D. Bachman; 27, Alexis Rosenfeld; 36, 43, Jeffrey Greenberg; 42, Ron Church.

Editor: Mary Perrotta Rich
Editorial Director: Michelle Bisson
Art Director: Anahid Hamparian
Series Designer: Adam Mietlowski

Printed in Malaysia

1 3 5 6 4 2

Contents

1 Living Fossils

A painted turtle crawls from the mud at the bottom of a pond onto a log to bask in the warmth of the morning sun. Nearby, a young raccoon patrolling the edge of the water spots the turtle and hopes to capture it for a meal. Sensing danger, the turtle expels all the air from its lungs with a long hiss. The turtle now has room inside its shell to safely draw in its legs, tail, and head. Grabbing the turtle, the raccoon attempts to pry the shell apart. The shell is strong and protects the turtle. Frustrated, the inexperienced raccoon flips the turtle onto its back and returns to the woods. The turtle is lucky this time.

These eastern painted turtles are soaking up the summer sun.

This Florida box turtle will have to work hard to right itself.

After a short while the turtle pokes its head and front legs out of its shell. It wriggles and pushes against the ground with its head. Using its strong neck muscles and front legs, it flips itself upright and then crawls back into the pond and settles in the mud at the bottom.

Turtles and tortoises are *ectotherms*. They regulate their own body temperature. If a turtle needs warmth, it seeks sunshine or warm pockets of shallow water. If a turtle needs to cool off, it must rest in shade or immerse itself in colder water. Turtles and tortoises sometimes bury themselves in mud. They have a thick covering of *scales* that protects their skin. This means they are *reptiles* just like snakes, crocodiles, and lizards.

The turtles that are swimming are cooling off while those on the bank are warming themselves.

There are more than two hundred fifty different types of turtles and tortoises living in the world today. These fascinating creatures live on every continent of the world except Antarctica, where it is too cold for them to survive. Two-thirds of all turtles are freshwater turtles. They are found in ponds, marshes, swamps, streams, and lakes. One-third of all turtles are sea turtles. There are eight different species of sea turtle that live in the oceans around the world. The rest of the animals we think of as turtles live on land and are known as tortoises.

An alligator snapping turtle, the largest species of freshwater turtle, has a pink appendage on its tongue that lures fish right to its mouth.

See how tiny the speckled padloper is next to one of the world's largest species, the Aldabra tortoise.

Tortoises have large, domed shells and strong, thick legs. Most weigh less than 10 pounds (4.5 kilograms), but some are big and quite heavy. The Galapagos Islands off the west coast of South America are home to many huge tortoises. Giant Galapagos tortoises can weigh more than 500 pounds (226.8 kilograms). One of these tortoises lived in *captivity* at the San Diego Zoo in California. At its heaviest, it weighed 681 pounds (308.9 kilograms).

Tortoises have a reputation for moving very slowly, as described in the famous fable "The Tortoise and the

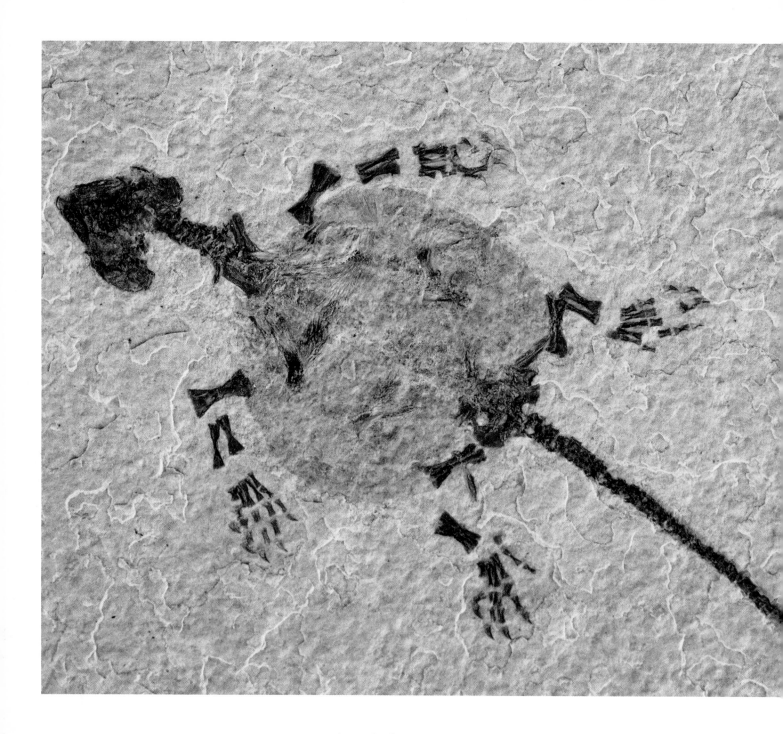

A turtle fossil

Hare." In one day a tortoise can travel only 7 miles (about 11.3 kilometers). In comparison, a swift sea turtle, aided by strong ocean currents, can swim more than 20 miles (32 kilometers) per hour.

Turtles and tortoises come in all sizes. The smallest is the speckled padloper from South Africa whose shell is only 3 inches across. The largest is the leatherback sea turtle. This massive creature can be more than 6 feet (1.8 meters) long and weigh up to 2,000 pounds (about 907.2 kilograms).

Turtles have lived on Earth for more than 200 million years. Prehistoric sea turtles existed alongside dinosaurs. Scientists have found the skeletons of an ancient species of sea turtle known as the Archelon turtle that are 10 feet (3.1 meters) long. This giant turtle was as large as a small car and weighed 2 tons (2 metric tons).

Other than in size, turtles have changed very little since prehistoric times. This is why they are sometimes referred to as living fossils. Turtles and tortoises are fascinating creatures, and humans are discovering more about them as they continue to study them in the wild and in captivity.

**Did
You Know . . .**
Turtles are physically unable to stick their tongues out of their mouths.

2 A Shell for a Home

Turtles are the only *vertebrates* with a hard shell. This shell is attached to the turtle's rib cage and backbone. A turtle cannot leave its shell; the shell grows as the turtle grows. The top part of the shell is called the *carapace*. The bottom part is known as the *plastron*. Both are connected by a bony bridge on either side of the turtle.

The shell is made of bones covered by scaly plates called *scutes*. A typical turtle shell has 38 scutes making up the carapace and 12 scutes in the plastron. Scutes are made of *keratin*, the same material that forms human fingernails.

You can see the flat shell and large flippers of the hawksbill turtle as it swims over a coral reef.

The leopard tortoise has a beautiful domed shell.

Scutes grow outward as a turtle ages much like the rings of a tree trunk. But it is not possible to tell the exact age of a turtle by examining its scutes. The width of the scutes increases during years when food is plentiful and temperatures are warm. During colder than usual seasons, if food is scarce or the turtle has been ill, scutes are narrow.

Sea turtles have flatter, more flexible shells than tortoises or freshwater turtles. Some turtles do not have any scutes at all. Leatherback, pig-nose, and soft-shell turtles have a thick, leathery skin rather than scutes.

Turtle and tortoise shells vary greatly, and many have elaborate markings and patterns. Some are unusually beautiful. But shells are not just decorative, they protect the animal from *predators* and the

The matamata turtle is hardly noticeable.

15

The light colored plastron of the hawksbill turtle helps keep it hidden from predators below it in the wate

environment. If anything touches a turtle's shell, the turtle can feel the pressure. The large, domed shell of a tortoise protects it from the hot sun. When turtles or tortoises withdraw into their shells, predators have a more difficult time harming them. Some turtle shells are so strong that a 200-pound (90.7 kilogram) person can stand on one and not damage it at all.

Shells also provide good *camouflage*, helping the turtle blend in with its surroundings. The South American matamata turtle has a reddish brown shell and loose flaps of skin that resemble dead leaves on its head and legs. This makes the turtle nearly invisible when it rests at the bottom of a pond. When a fish swims near a matamata, the turtle opens its large mouth and sucks in the fish.

Sea turtles also have special coloring to disguise them in ocean waters. The carapace is a dark color that blends in with the water and helps hide the turtle from flying birds searching the water for food. The plastron is a lighter color that blends in with the sky, hiding the turtle from predators swimming below and looking upward. This particular type of camouflage is known as "countershading."

Did You Know . . . The flesh, skin, and skeleton of a leatherback turtle is full of natural oils that protect the animal from the sea. Long ago, this oil was used in lamps, much like whale oil.

17

These three sea turtles can move through the water quite easily.

Like other reptiles, turtles and tortoises shed their skins. Unlike snakes, which shed their skin all at once, turtles shed theirs in small flaky patches as new scales grow. Their rough, scaly skin protects the parts of the animal that stick out of its shell. Tortoises have particularly tough skin on their feet and legs. When a tortoise is in danger, it uses its flat, shovellike front legs to cover its face like a shield.

Freshwater turtles have webbing between their toes to help them swim. Sea turtles, instead of having separate toes, have big flippers that make them powerful swimmers. These turtles glide gracefully through the water and cover amazing distances.

On land, most turtles and tortoises move slowly and awkwardly. Their shoulders and hips are inside their shells, making their legs stick straight out from their sides. Carrying the weight of their shells also slows them down. The heavy shell and unusual bone placement may seem like a disadvantage, but having a shell for a home has helped turtles survive for millions of years.

3 The Life Cycle of a Turtle

Two giant Galapagos tortoises meet in the hot sun of a spring day. Mating season has begun, and both are interested in the same female. They stretch their long necks and glare at each other. The turtle that can raise his head the highest wins the chance of mating.

In the desert, two male desert tortoises repeatedly charge each other, banging their shells together, each attempting to push the other one over. It is mating season, and the conflict centers around a female tortoise. If one tortoise ends up on his back, he loses more than the opportunity to mate—he may lose his life. Teetering on its back, a tortoise has trouble reaching the ground to push itself upright. If a tortoise cannot right itself

These Galapagos tortoises show their aggressive side by opening their mouths and holding their heads high.

The male desert tortoise (left) shows his interest in a female (right) by wagging his head at her.

and remains stranded on its back, it will not last long in the hot sun.

In ocean waters, a male sea turtle swims around and around a female turtle in a mating ritual that is millions of years old. The male gently bumps against the female and nibbles her legs and neck to show his interest. This underwater dance may go on for hours before mating occurs.

Once a female mates she must find a safe place to lay her eggs. Freshwater turtles and land tortoises dig a nest close to where they live, unless their *habitat* is in some way not good for the eggs. Sea turtles have an overpowering urge to *migrate* back to the beach where they were born. This journey can be as long as 3,000 miles (4,828 kilometers). Scientists are not sure how

These sea turtles are searching for mates off the coast of Malaysia.

An eastern box turtle lays eggs in its habitat.

sea turtles are able to locate their birthplace. Some think turtles may have an internal magnetic device, much like a compass, that senses Earth's magnetic pull. Sea turtles may also be able to detect familiar

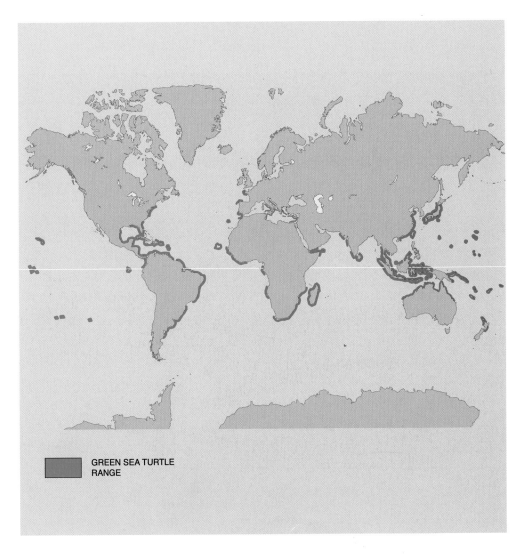

Green sea turtles live in many areas.

GREEN SEA TURTLE RANGE

smells carried on the ocean's currents. Somehow, the turtle returns to the beach where it hatched and pulls itself slowly across the sand using its flippers.

Next the sea turtle must find a place for a nest. With its back flippers, it digs a pit about 2 feet (0.6 meter) deep. This will help keep the eggs safe from

A green sea turtle uses its rear flippers to dig an egg-laying pit.

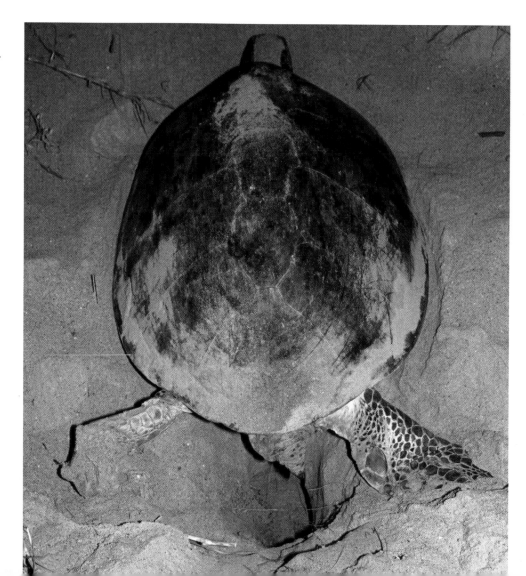

*The turtle eggs found in a nest on a beach look a lot like
Ping-Pong balls!*

predators and any tides that might rise up onto
the beach. The turtle lays eighty to two hundred Ping-Pong-ball-sized eggs. This is
known as a *clutch*. Females lay an average of
four clutches per season. After the eggs are
deposited, the turtle covers them up with
sand and lies on top of the nest to compact it
with the weight of her body. She then heads
back to the sea, never seeing the nest again.

27

Here is a rare and endangered leatherback sea turtle hatchling.

The sun-warmed sand *incubates* the eggs and keeps them warm. The temperature of the nest determines if the *hatchlings* will be male or female. Warmer temperatures produce females; cooler nests produce males. If the top of the nest is warmer, females will develop there and males will develop below. It takes about forty-five to seventy days before the hatchlings are ready to crack through their shells using their egg tooth at the end of their nose.

Once they emerge from their shells, it can take up to three days for the hatchlings to crawl up through the sand to the surface. They work together as a group, allowing the sand to fill the empty nest chamber behind them. Then they begin a dangerous journey to the ocean. The hatchlings' shells, soft and barely the size of a quarter, provide no protection. Predators such as sea birds, crabs, raccoons, snakes, and wild pigs can easily grab up the tiny turtles. Once in the water, hatchlings are *prey* to fish and sharks. It is estimated that only one in a thousand sea turtles lives to adulthood.

Young sea turtles swim in seaweed, which helps to hide them. For the first year of life, they eat *plankton*, or tiny plants and animals that float on the ocean's surface. Turtles grow quickly, and by the end of their first year, their shells are the size of dinner plates. The turtles then venture into other waters, sometimes to forage around reefs.

Freshwater turtles and tortoises do not mate until they are ten to twenty years old. Some sea turtle species will even wait for twenty to fifty years before beginning their own families. Since turtles live long lives, females can lay thousands of eggs over their lifetimes.

Did You Know . . .

Tortoises don't always produce eggs right after mating. In rare instances a turtle will lay eggs up to three years later.

4 A Gentle Existence

Most turtles are gentle creatures. Their days are spent resting and eating. When threatened, their first instinct is to retreat inside their shells. Pulling their heads inside is an interesting process. Straight-neck turtles pull their heads backward, and their necks bend into an "S" formation with their head resting at the bottom of the "S." Side-neck turtles pull their heads to one side as their name implies. Sea turtles cannot pull their bodies inside their shells, so they must swim quickly to evade predators.

Musk turtles have a particularly smelly defense mechanism. Like a skunk, they have powerful scent glands. When threatened they emit a foul-smelling

The defensive posture of the eastern box turtle seems more passive than combative.

substance from the bridge of their shell, which is the reason they are also known as stinkpot turtles.

Snapping turtles are the most dangerous of the species. Alligator snapping turtles have a flap of skin on their tongues that wiggles and looks like a small fish. This built-in lure attracts fish, and when the fish swim up to the snapping turtle, the turtle clamps down and captures its meal. Their powerful jaws are built to

Nobody would want this snapping turtle to bite down on him or her!

This turtle is enjoying a meal of strawberries.

snap food in half, which they then swallow. Although shy by nature, snapping turtles can be aggressive if provoked by animals or humans and will clamp down on an attacker and hang on.

Turtles are *omnivorous*, which means they eat both plants and animals. They have no teeth. Their jaws develop a hard ridge that makes them appear to have a beak, which they use to crush, cut, and tear their food. Turtles eat plants, insects, worms, and snails. The diet of desert tortoises includes cactus, native grasses, and desert vines.

The front limbs of the gopher tortoise are especially good for digging.

Sea turtles eat sea grasses, crabs, oysters, sponges, and even coral. The giant leatherback's favorite food is jellyfish. Sea turtles consume large quantities of salt from all the seawater they drink. If they have too much salt in their bodies they can die. To get rid of the excess salt, they shed big, salty tears.

Turtles generally live solitary lives, but a gopher tortoise shares its home with other animals. Gopher tortoises are about 1 foot (30.5 centimeters) long, but they dig underground burrows that can be 30 feet (9.1 meters) long or longer. Other animals such as gophers, snakes, rabbits, mice, lizards, and toads move into these tunnels, and they all happily share the space.

Another unusual characteristic of turtles is their ability to *hibernate* during the cold winter months. Although they do not go into a deep sleep, some turtles will bury themselves in mud and not move for two to three months. Their body functions slow down. They live off the fat that is stored in their bodies. When warmer weather arrives, they emerge from the mud hungry but healthy.

5 Endangered

Turtles and tortoises have many natural predators, but humans are their greatest threat. Many species of turtle are labeled as *endangered*. Some are listed as "high risk." This means that unless something is done to protect them, experts believe they will be extinct in as little as twenty years. Some species have been reduced in number by the thousands over the last two hundred years. For example, the giant Galapagos tortoises once thrived on the Galapagos Islands. However, they were hunted to near extinction and now number less than fifteen thousand. There are currently laws in place that protect these tortoises, and hopefully their numbers will increase.

Laws now protect the giant Galapagos tortoises from being hunted.

The first known turtle conservation law went into effect in 1620 on the island of Bermuda. Eating sea turtles was popular then, and they were being killed at an alarming rate. The law prohibited the killing of turtles that were smaller than 18 inches (46 centimeters) across. The fine for breaking this law was 15 pounds (6.8 kilograms) of tobacco, a highly prized

These women are packing turtle eggs to be sold.

crop. In the late 1970s a strong animal conservation movement began. Although laws prohibiting the slaughter of turtles now exist worldwide, turtles are still killed and eaten all the time.

Even with protective laws in place, *poaching* continues. Humans raid turtle nests for the eggs. They also kill turtles and sell the body parts for food. In Asian countries various turtle parts are used in medicine. Turtles are also killed for their shells, which are made into jewelry and decorative items. Breeders export turtles as pets. Many die during transport from dehydration, and nearly all become sick. Some are later abandoned by their owners once they grow larger.

Pollution is another major problem that poses a severe threat to turtles. Leatherbacks choke to death on discarded plastic bags they mistake for jellyfish. Other sea turtles sometimes eat discarded cigarette butts, mistaking them for small fish floating in the water. The toxins in cigarettes remain in their bodies and can make the turtles sick.

Some sea turtles in Florida suffer from fibropapillomatosis, a disease that causes wartlike *tumors* to grow on the turtle's body. These tumors can cluster around the turtle's face, making it difficult for the turtle to eat and see. If the tumors cluster on the flippers, they can interfere with swimming. Some turtles die from the disease. Experts think that fibropapillomatosis may be linked to pollution. The disease has also been observed in sea turtles in Hawaii.

Light pollution from large hotels located on beaches is also a cause for concern. After nesting, turtles look for the light that reflects off the sea to find their way back to the ocean. They can become confused by hotel lights and go in the wrong direction, getting killed in traffic and facing other hazards. Some beachfront communities are making laws prohibiting hotels from having large amounts of light at night during nesting season.

Destruction of natural habitat due to land development also endangers turtles. Safe nesting sites and breeding grounds for turtles are being destroyed. Sandbags and other man-made barriers erected to prevent beach erosion also prevent turtles from coming inland to nest. Large machines rake and clean public beaches, and the sand is not as deep as it would be naturally. This makes it difficult

Here's an unusual warning sign on Sanibel Island, Florida.

for turtles to dig nests that are deep enough. The compacted sand is also a problem for young hatchlings trying to dig their way out of the nest. In some areas *conservationists* monitor nesting turtles and even move their eggs to a safer spot if necessary.

Many turtles die when they are caught in shrimping nets. Since 1989, U.S. law requires shrimp boats of a certain size or larger to use turtle excluder devices (TEDs). These devices give turtles a built-in escape door to swim out of the nets and prevent drowning. Unfortunately, sometimes the devices are

This sea turtle is caught in a fishing net.

The Turtle Hospital in the Florida Keys rescues, rehabilitates, and releases turtles back into the local environment.

removed in the mistaken belief that doing so will lead to bigger shrimp catches.

Conservationists all over the world continue to fight for laws that protect turtles and tortoises. They hope to stop the pollution and development that threaten the reptiles' habitats. They are striving to put an end to illegal poaching. They continue to work to protect known breeding grounds. With worldwide cooperation, endangered turtle and tortoise populations should recover and thrive.

Glossary

camouflage: Having an appearance that makes something blend in with its surroundings.

captivity: Kept confined, as in a zoo.

carapace: The top part of a turtle shell.

clutch: A group of turtle eggs laid at one time.

conservationists: People who help preserve and protect wildlife.

ectotherm: An animal that regulates its body temperature by moving to areas that have the warmth or coolness it needs.

endangered: Threatened with extinction.

habitat: The place where an animal lives.

hatchlings: A newly hatched reptile, fish, bird, or amphibian.

hibernate: To sleep through the winter.

incubate: To keep something warm.

keratin: A strong material that forms the claws, scales, and scutes of a turtle.

migrate: To travel from one territory to another.

omnivorous: Eating both plants and animals.

plankton: Tiny plants and animals that float on the ocean's surface.

plastron: The bottom part of a turtle shell.

poaching: To hunt or fish in a forbidden area.

pollution: The dirty or harmful condition of water, air, or soil.

predator: An animal that hunts another animal.

prey: An animal that is hunted by another animal.

reptiles: Crawling or creeping animals that have scales and are ectotherms.

scales: A reptile's strong, hard skin covering.

scutes: The scaly covering of a turtle's shell.

tumors: An abnormal growth of cells in an animal.

vertebrate: An animal that has a backbone.

Find Out More

Books

Becker, John E. *Green Sea Turtles*. San Diego: Kidhaven Press, 2004.

Biel, Timothy Levi. *Turtles*. San Diego: Wildlife Education, Ltd., 1993.

Cooper, Jason. *Loggerhead Turtle*. Vero Beach, FL: Rourke Publishing, 2003.

Jacobs, Lee. *Turtles*. San Diego: Blackbirch Press, 2003.

Kalman, Bobbie. *Endangered Sea Turtles*. New York: Crabtree Publishing, 2004.

——. *The Life Cycle of a Sea Turtle*. New York: Crabtree Publishing, 2002.

Martin-James, Kathleen. *Sturdy Turtles*. Minneapolis: Lerner Publications, 2000.

Schafer, Susan. *The Galapagos Tortoise*. New York: Dillon Press, 1992.

Trueit, Trudi. *Turtles*. New York: Children's Press, 2003.

Web Sites

Caribbean Conservation Corporation and Sea Turtle Survival League
www.cccturtle.org

Tortoise Trust
www.tortoisetrust.org

Turtle Trax
www.turtles.org

About the Author

Renee C. Rebman has published several nonfiction books for young readers. She is also a published playwright. Her plays have been produced in schools and community theaters across the country.

Index

Page numbers for illustrations are in **boldface**.